Boost Your Score
Underground Calculator
Programs for the ACT Test

Thanks for your purchase! Here's the fine print: We are not endorsed by the makers of the ACT. You are responsible to validate the formulas and programs in this book and in your calculator. Advantage Point assumes no responsibility for errors in formulas or malfunctions of the calculator during a test. You should review ACT's rules for calculator use before using these programs on each test you take. ACT, Inc. can change calculator rules at any time. Also, to avoid accidentally clearing your calculator's memory, replace your batteries BEFORE adding these programs. A total memory-wipeout with battery replacement is very, very uncommon but we have seen it happen!

Good luck!

Boost Your Score
Underground Calculator Programs for the ACT Test

adv∧ntagePoint
cutting edge test prep | painless prices

ISBN-13 978-0-615-43593-0
ISBN-10 0-6154-3593-9

CONTENTS

PART II
Calculator Tips and Tricks

INTRODUCTION

Use your calculator, not your brain!

WELL...SOMETIMES.

Congratulations! You've stumbled on a tool that can help you easily boost your ACT math score by two points or more. We have been using ACT calculator programs with our ACT prep students with great results and have finally decided to release these easy-to-use programs for public use. This packet is a collection of the TI calculator programs that are both extremely easy to program (even for the tech-phobic) and most helpful on the ACT.

Believe it or not, there are no rules banning the use of calculator programs stored in your TI 83 or 84 on the ACT. So why not follow these simple programming instructions and have your calculator calculate time-consuming equations like the distance formula and quadratic formula for you? Using these programs will improve your accuracy and free up time for you – time you can now shift over to other problems you may not be able to tackle otherwise.

On the June 2010 ACT, there were 7 different opportunities to use these programs. What a timesaver! We found there were fewer possibilities on the October ACT (only 5), but the time saved using these programs still helped enormously with student pacing and accuracy.

As a bonus to help you practice using these programs on real tests, we've highlighted some opportunities to use these calculator programs on the 3 official tests in The Real ACT Prep Guide (available at your local library or on Amazon) and on the free official ACT test located here on the ACT website: *http://www.act.org/aap/preparing.pdf.* You'll see these test questions noted throughout this booklet.

We are a small test prep company and we love to hear from our students! If you have any programs to add or any you wish to see added, please drop us a line. We are also always available for support or cheerleading. You can reach us at *contact@ advantagepointonline.com.*

Ready? Here is a list of calculator programs that can save you time on the ACT. Program them into your TI 83 or 84. (Note that the TI-89 is permitted on the SAT but is not permitted on the ACT). Then make sure to practice, practice, practice to make sure you are completely comfortable using them on test day!

Good luck!

THE ADVANTAGE POINT TEAM

Before you get started:

- **Please note that you still need to have a basic understanding of these math concepts to use your calculator effectively.** For example, for a program to quickly calculate the area of a circle, your calculator will need to prompt you for the circle's radius. Therefore, you still need to know how to locate the radius of a circle even though your calculator can do the rest for you.

- Remember that you have a limited amount of memory on your calculator. If you find your calculator is slowing down, you may need to delete some programs.

- For maximum efficiency, we recommend that you only input the programs you feel will be truly helpful to you. For example, if you are a student who can quickly calculate the area or circumference of a circle by hand, you may not want to program these programs into your calculator. This will free you up on test day to quickly locate the programs you really need on your programs list.

PART I

Programs to input by hand

CHAPTER 1

Pythagorean Theorem when the hypotenuse is missing

You've probably already noticed that the ACT folks love right triangles. This program will find the hypotenuse of a right triangle using the Pythagorean Theorem. You will be prompted to input the other two sides of the triangle.

STEP-BY-STEP DIRECTIONS

1. Hit [**PGRM**] and slide over to select NEW. Hit [**ENTER**].

2. Give the new program a name like PYTHAG and hit [**ENTER**]

3. Hit [**PGRM**], slide over to I/O, and select Prompt

4. Hit [**ALPHA**] and A, B. Hit [**ENTER**].

5. Put in the formula $\sqrt{(A^2 + B^2)}$. (Use the [**ALPHA**] button to input the letters in the equation). Then hit the [**STO**] button (right above the ON button). After the little arrow, hit [**ALPHA**] and type in a C. Hit [**ENTER**].

6. Go to [**PGRM**], slide over to I/O and choose Disp. Then put a C.

7. Hit [**2nd**] and then [**MODE**] to quit setup. Go to [**PGRM**] and EXEC and choose it from your program list to use it.

WHAT YOUR SCREEN SHOULD LOOK LIKE WHEN PROGRAMMING

```
PROGRAM:PYTHAG
:Prompt A,B
:√(A²+B²)→C
:Disp C
:■
```

SEE IT ON A SAMPLE ACT QUESTION:

1. The foot of a ladder is placed 9 feet from a wall. If the top of the ladder rests 12 feet up on the wall, how many feet long is the ladder?

   A. 9

   B. $9\sqrt{2}$

   C. 10

   D. 15

   E. $15\sqrt{2}$

Note: The ACT folks love this type of problem! Did you realize this is a right triangle problem in disguise? You can take the time to do the Pythagorean Theorem by hand… or you can let your calculator solve this problem in a matter of seconds.

Hit the [**PGRM**] button, select PYTHAG, and you will be prompted for A and B, the two legs of the right triangle. Here, A = 9, B = 12 (or vice-versa). The calculator will give you 15, the hypotenuse. The correct answer is D.

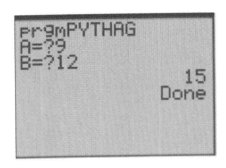

2. If right triangle ABC is isosceles, what is the approximate length of x in inches?

A. 5

B. 6

C. 7

D. 8

E. 9

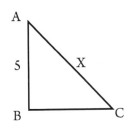

Note: Since this is an isosceles triangle, both of the short legs are 5 inches long. Since you are told this is a right triangle, you can use the Pythagorean Theorem.

Hit the [**PGRM**] button, select PYTHAG, and you will be prompted for A and B, the two legs of the right triangle. Here, A = 5 and B = 5. The calculator will give you 7.07, the hypotenuse. The correct answer is C.

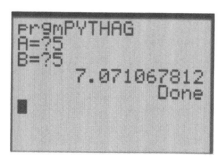

Do you have The Real ACT Prep Guide (2005 or 2007) or the free practice test from the ACT website (2009-2012)? Check out these opportunities to use this program:

Real ACT Prep Guide Test 1: #20, #25

Real ACT Prep Guide Test 2: #31 (to test answers), #33, #48, #52

CHAPTER 2

Pythagorean Theorem when one of the smaller legs is missing

You've probably already noticed that the ACT and SAT folks love right triangles. This program will find one of the shorter (non-hypotenuse) legs of a right triangle using the Pythagorean Theorem. You will be prompted to input the other leg and the hypotenuse.

STEP-BY-STEP DIRECTIONS

1. Hit [**PGRM**] and slide over to select NEW. Hit [**ENTER**].

2. Give the new program a name like PYTHLEG and hit [**ENTER**]

3. Hit [**PGRM**], slide over to I/O, and select Prompt

4. Hit [**ALPHA**] and A, C. Hit [**ENTER**].

5. Put in the formula $\sqrt{(C^2 - A^2)}$ Then hit the [**STO**] button (right above the ON button). After the little arrow, hit [**ALPHA**] and type in a B. Hit [**ENTER**].

6. Go to [**PGRM**], slide over to I/O and choose Disp. Then put a B.

7. Hit [**2nd**] and then [**MODE**] to quit setup. Go to [**PGRM**] and EXEC and choose it from your program list to use it.

WHAT YOUR SCREEN SHOULD LOOK LIKE WHEN PROGRAMMING

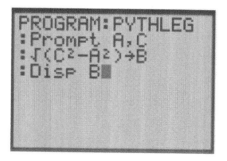

```
PROGRAM:PYTHLEG
:Prompt A,C
:√(C²-A²)→B
:Disp B
```

SEE IT ON A SAMPLE ACT QUESTION:

1. Jacob's TV screen is 20 inches long. If the diagonal of the screen measures 25 inches, what is the width of Jacob's TV?

   A. 10

   B. $10\sqrt{2}$

   C. 12

   D. 15

   E. $15\sqrt{2}$

Note: Again, this is a right triangle problem in disguise. (If you're a visual learner, you may want to draw a picture). You can take the time to do the Pythagorean Theorem by hand... or you can let your calculator do the dirty work.

Hit the [**PGRM**] button, select PYTHLEG, and you will be prompted for A and C, the short leg of the right triangle and the hypotenuse. Here, A = 20 and C = 25. The calculator will give you 15, the other leg. The correct answer is D.

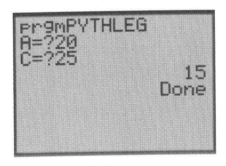

2. In the figure below, what is the value of x?

A. $2\sqrt{3}$

B. 5

C. $5\sqrt{2}$

D. $5\sqrt{3}$

E. $10\sqrt{3}$

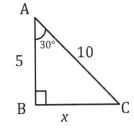

Note: If you know the 30-60-90 side ratios, by all means, use those! Otherwise, head to this calculator program to find the missing leg. Keep in mind, however, that your calculator will return the answer in a decimal. You will then have to quickly eyeball or test the answers to match up the decimal to the right answer in radical form.

Hit the [**PGRM**] button, select PYTHLEG, and you will be prompted for A and C, the short leg of the right triangle and the hypotenuse. Here, A = 5 and C = 10. The calculator will give you 8.66, the other leg. Hopefully, by quickly "eyeball-ing" the answer choices, you can narrow the answer to answer choice D.

Do you have The Real ACT Prep Guide (2005 or 2007) or the free practice test from the ACT website (2009-2012)? Check out these opportunities to use this program:

Free practice test (on ACT website): #38

Real ACT Prep Guide Test 1: #37

Real ACT Prep Guide Test 3: #4, #41

CHAPTER 3

Distance formula

This program will compute the distance between two points. This is a huge timesaver on the ACT and great for students who don't remember how to use the distance formula.

For this program, the two sets of points are (A,B) (C, D). After trying these programs with thousands of students, we've found that when students are working quickly on test day, the (A, B) (C, D) system is much easier than having to keep track of x_1, x_2, y_1, and y_2. You'll see—just give this a try.

Plug the numbers into your calculator from left to right as it prompts you for A, B, C, and D. To use this program, the set of points are (A, B) (C, D). Your calculator will give you the distance between those points.

STEP-BY-STEP DIRECTIONS

1. Hit [**PGRM**] and slide over to select NEW. Hit [**ENTER**].

2. Give the new program a name like DISTANCE and hit [**ENTER**].

3. Hit [**PGRM**], slide over to I/O, and select Prompt.

4. Hit [**ALPHA**] and the letters A,B, C, D. Hit [**ENTER**].

5. Put in the formula $\sqrt{((a-c)^2 + (b-d)^2)}$. Then hit the [**STO**] button (right above the ON button). After the little arrow, hit [**ALPHA**] and type in an E. Hit [**ENTER**].

6. Go to [**PGRM**], slide over to I/O and choose Disp. Then put an E.

7. Hit [**2nd**] and then [**MODE**] to quit setup. Go to [**PGRM**] and EXEC and choose it from your program list to use it.

WHAT YOUR SCREEN SHOULD LOOK LIKE WHEN PROGRAMMING

```
PROGRAM:DISTANCE
:Prompt A,B,C,D
:√((A-C)²+(B-D)²
)→E
:Disp E
:█
```

SEE IT ON A SAMPLE ACT QUESTION:

1. What is the distance between $(-4, 10)$ and $(5, -2)$?

A. 6

B. 9

C. 10

D. 12

E. 15

Note: When you're working quickly on the ACT, it's hard to keep track of what's x_1, x_2, y_1, and y_2. Don't worry about it. Just plug the numbers into your calculator from left to right as it prompts you for A, B, C, and D. Hit the [**PGRM**] button, select DISTANCE, and you will be prompted for A, B, C, and D. Here, A = -4, B = 10, C = 5, and D = -2. The calculator will give you 15, the distance between the two points. The answer choice is E.

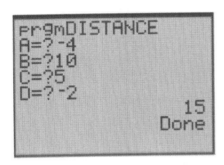

2. What is the distance between $(3\sqrt{3}, 6)$ and $(5\sqrt{3}, 12)$?

A. 3

B. $4\sqrt{3}$

C. 6

D. $6\sqrt{3}$

E. 8

Note: It's unusual to see a distance problem this obnoxious on the ACT, but it happens. If you see one, you'll be prepared. Just plug the numbers into your calculator from left to right as it prompts you for A, B, C, and D. Hit the [**PGRM**] button, select DISTANCE, and you will be prompted for A, B, C, and D. Here, A = $3\sqrt{3}$, B = 6, C = $5\sqrt{3}$, and D = 12. Remember that the calculator will give you a decimal if your answer is a radical. In this case, the calculator gives you 6.928, the distance between the two points. If you calculate answer choices B and D on your calculator, you'll see that B is the correct answer.

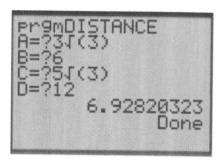

Do you have The Real ACT Prep Guide (2005 or 2007) or the free practice test from the ACT website (2009-2012)? Check out these opportunities to use this program:

Free practice test (on ACT website): #10 (to check answers), #37 (to check answers)

Real ACT Prep Guide Test 1: #45

Real ACT Prep Guide Test 3: #38

CHAPTER 4

Area of a circle

If you have trouble remembering the formula for the area of a circle, you may want to install this program. This program will compute the area of a circle if you plug in the radius. **Please note that the program will calculate the numerical value of π and will give you a decimal answer.**

STEP-BY-STEP DIRECTIONS

1. Hit [**PGRM**] and slide over to select NEW. Hit [**ENTER**].

2. Give the new program a name like ACIRC and hit [**ENTER**]

3. Hit [**PGRM**], slide over to I/O, and select Prompt

4. Hit [**ALPHA**] and the letter R. Hit [**ENTER**].

5. Put in the formula πR^2. Then hit the [**STO**] button (right above the ON button). After the little arrow, hit [**ALPHA**] and type in an A. Hit [**ENTER**].

6. Go to [**PGRM**], slide over to I/O and choose Disp. Then put an A.

7. Hit [**2nd**] and then [**MODE**] to quit setup. Go to [**PGRM**] and EXEC and choose it from your program list to use it.

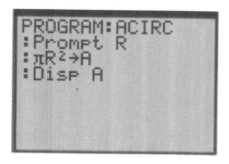

```
PROGRAM:ACIRC
:Prompt R
:πR²→A
:Disp A
```

SEE IT ON A SAMPLE ACT QUESTION:

1. A cellular phone tower broadcasts a signal for 25 miles in all directions. Which of the following is closest to the area, in square miles, of the circle that represents the signal coverage of the tower?

   A. 25

   B. 145

   C. 1964

   D. 3566

   E. 7853

Note: Since the signal is emitted from a tower and extends for 25 miles in every direction, the radius of the circle representing cellular coverage is 25.

If I hit the [**PGRM**] button and select the program ACIRC, I am prompted for R, the radius. The calculator then gives me the area of the circle – 1963.495. The answer is C.

2. A circle is inscribed in a square as shown below. If the area of the square is 16, what is the area of the circle?

A. 2

B. 2π

C. 4π

D. 8π

E. 16π

Note: This is a tricky one. Since the circle is inscribed inside the square, the side of each square is equal to the diameter of the circle. (If you're a visual learner, you may want to draw this). Since the area of the square is 16, each of the sides of the square is 4. That means that the diameter of the circle is 4 and the radius of the circle is 2, half the diameter.

If I hit the [**PGRM**] button and select the program ACIRC, I am prompted for R, the radius. The calculator then gives me the area of the circle – 12.56. Remember that your calculator just multiplied the π into your answer. Hopefully, by 'eyeball-ing' or testing the answer choices, you'll notice that 12.566 = 4π.

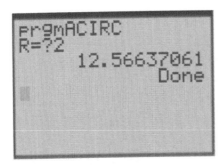

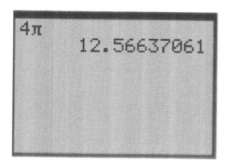

Do you have The Real ACT Prep Guide (2005 or 2007) or the free practice test from the ACT website (2009-2012)? Check out these opportunities to use this program:

Free practice test (on ACT website): #54

Real ACT Prep Guide Test 2: #30, #52

Real ACT Prep Guide Test 3: #51

CHAPTER 5

Solve a quadratic equation

On the ACT you will certainly see one or more questions asking you to find the solutions/roots for quadratic equations. These are equations with the form $ax^2+bx+c = 0$. (If you're rusty, check out the sample problems. Hopefully those questions will jog your memory.) This program finds the solutions as long as you input the coefficient of each part of the quadratic: a, b, and c. If there is no coefficient in front of the x^2, be sure to put a 1.

STEP-BY-STEP DIRECTIONS

1. Hit [**PGRM**] and slide over to select NEW. Hit [**ENTER**].

2. Give the new program a name like QUAD and hit [**ENTER**]

3. Hit [**PGRM**], slide over to I/O, and select Prompt

4. Hit [**ALPHA**] and [**ENTER**] A, B, C (your comma button is next to your parenthesis)

5. Put in the formula $(\text{-}B + \sqrt{(B^2 - 4AC)})/(2A)$. (Use the [**ALPHA**] button to input the letters in the equation). Then hit the [**STO**] button (right above the ON button). After the little arrow, hit [**ALPHA**] and type in a D.

6. Put in the formula $(^-B - \sqrt{(B^2 - 4AC)})/(2A)$. Then hit the [**STO**] button (right above the ON button). After the little arrow, hit [**ALPHA**] and type in an E. Hit [**ENTER**].

7. Go to [**PGRM**], slide over to I/O and choose Disp. Then put D, E.

8. Hit [**2nd**] and then [**MODE**] to quit setup. Go to [**PGRM**] and EXEC and choose it from your program list to use it.

WHAT YOUR SCREEN SHOULD LOOK LIKE WHEN PROGRAMMING

```
PROGRAM:QUAD
:Prompt A,B,C
:(-B+√(B²-4AC))/
(2A)→D
:(-B-√(B²-4AC))/
(2A)→E
:Disp D,E
```

SEE IT ON A SAMPLE ACT QUESTION:

1. What values of x are solutions for $2x^2 + 4x = 16$?

A. -4 and -2

B. 4 and 2

C. -4 and 2

D. -4 and 4

E. -4 and 8

Note: Yes, you can actually take the time to do this problem by hand... or you can let your calculator solve this problem in a matter of seconds.

Remember that to solve a quadratic equation (and to use this program), you need to set the equation equal to zero. So we need to move the equation around to get $2x^2 + 4x - 16 = 0$.

Then, hit the [**PGRM**] button, select QUAD, and you will be prompted for A, B, and C. Here, A = 2, B = 4, and C = -16. When you input these values, the calculator will give you the roots: 2 and -4. The answer is C.

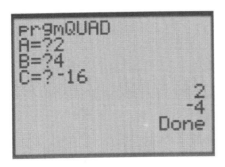

2. Which value of x is a root of $x^2 + 9x + 18 = 0$?

A. -3

B. 2

C. 3

D. 6

E. 9

Note: Again, you can take the time to do this problem by hand... or you can let your calculator solve this problem in seconds.

Hit the [**PGRM**] button, select QUAD, and you will be prompted for A, B, and C. Here, A = 1, B = 9, and C = 18. When you input these values, the calculator will give you the roots: -3 and -6. The correct answer is A.

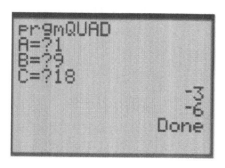

Do you have The Real ACT Prep Guide (2005 or 2007) or the free practice test from the ACT website (2009-2012)? Check out these opportunities to use this program:

Free practice test (on ACT website): #21

Real ACT Prep Guide Test 1: #23

CHAPTER 6

Find the slope when given two points

You will occasionally be asked to find the slope of a line when given two points. You can use the calculator technique mentioned in the Tips and Tricks section or use the program below.

For this program, the two sets of points are (A,B) (C, D). After trying these programs with thousands of students, we've found that when students are working quickly on test day, the (A, B) (C, D) system is much easier than having to keep track of x_1, x_2, y_1, and y_2. You'll see—just give this a try.

Plug the numbers into your calculator from left to right as it prompts you for A, B, C, and D. The program will display the slope.

STEP-BY-STEP DIRECTIONS

1. Hit [**PGRM**] and slide over to select NEW. Hit [**ENTER**].

2. Give the new program a name like SLOPE and hit [**ENTER**]

3. Hit [**PGRM**], slide over to I/O, and select Prompt

4. Hit [**ALPHA**] and the letters A,B,C,D. Hit [**ENTER**].

5. Put in the formula ((D-B)/(C-A)). Then hit the [**STO**] button (right above the ON button). After the little arrow, hit [**ALPHA**] and type in an E. Hit [**ENTER**].

6. Go to [**PGRM**], slide over to I/O and choose Disp. Then put an E.

7. Hit [**2nd**] and then [**MODE**] to quit setup. Go to [**PGRM**] and EXEC and choose it from your program list to use it.

WHAT YOUR SCREEN SHOULD LOOK LIKE WHEN PROGRAMMING

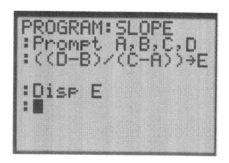

SEE IT ON A SAMPLE ACT QUESTION:

1. Line *l* passes through the points $(1, 3)$ and $(-2, -4)$. What is the reciprocal of the slope of *l*?

   A. $5/3$

   B. $2/5$

   C. $7/3$

   D. $3/7$

   E. $5/3$

Note: Hit the [**PGRM**] button, select SLOPE, and you will be prompted for A, B, C, and D. Here, A = 1, B = 3, C = -2, and D = -4. The calculator will return a decimal and give you 2.3333. To change the decimal into a fraction, hit MATH and then Frac to change your answer into a fraction. Since you are looking for the reciprocal, the answer choice is D.

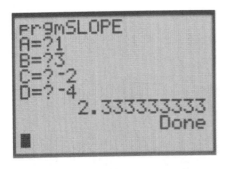

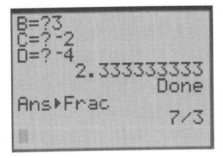

Do you have The Real ACT Prep Guide (2005 or 2007) or the free practice test from the ACT website (2009-2012)? Check out these opportunities to use this program:

Free practice test (on ACT website): #52

CHAPTER 7

Diagonals in a polygon

Several recent ACTs have included a question requiring students to find the number of diagonals in a polygon. This program will find the number of diagonals in a polygon with n sides when you input the number of sides.

STEP-BY-STEP DIRECTIONS

1. Hit [**PGRM**] and slide over to select NEW. Hit [**ENTER**].

2. Give the new program a name like DIAGONAL and hit [**ENTER**]

3. Hit [**PGRM**], slide over to I/O, and select Prompt

4. Hit [**ALPHA**] and the letter S. Hit [**ENTER**].

5. Put in the formula $(s(s-3))/2$. Then hit the [**STO**] button (right above the ON button). After the little arrow, hit [**ALPHA**] and type in a D. Hit [**ENTER**].

6. Go to [**PGRM**], slide over to I/O and choose Disp. Then put a D.

7. Hit [**2nd**] and then [**MODE**] to quit setup. Go to [**PGRM**] and EXEC and choose it from your program list to use it.

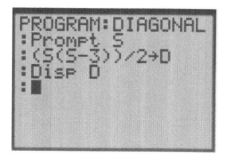

```
PROGRAM:DIAGONAL
:Prompt S
:(S(S-3))/2→D
:Disp D
:█
```

SEE IT ON A SAMPLE ACT QUESTION:

1. What is the maximum number of distinct diagonals that can be drawn in the figure below?

   A. 6

   B. 8

   C. 9

   D. 12

   E. 18

Note: While the person next to you spends three minutes frantically drawing diagonals, you can smirk and whip out this program.

Hit the [**PGRM**] button, select DIAGONAL, and you will be prompted for S, the amount of sides. Here, S = 6. The calculator will give you 9, the number of diagonals in a hexagon. The answer choice is C.

Do you have The Real ACT Prep Guide (2005 or 2007) or the free practice test from the ACT website (2009-2012)? Check out these opportunities to use this program:

Real ACT Prep Guide Test 1: #52

CHAPTER 8

Find the midpoint of a line when given two endpoints

You will occasionally be asked to find the midpoint of a line when given two points.

For this program, the two sets of points are (A,B) (C, D). After trying these programs with thousands of students, we've found that when students are working quickly on test day, the (A, B) (C, D) system is much easier than having to keep track of x_1, x_2, y_1, and y_2. You'll see—just give this a try.

Plug the numbers into your calculator from left to right as it prompts you for A, B, C, and D. The program will display the x and y coordinates of the midpoint.

STEP-BY-STEP DIRECTIONS

1. Hit [**PGRM**] and slide over to select NEW. Hit [**ENTER**].

2. Give the new program a name like MIDPT and hit [**ENTER**]

3. Hit [**PGRM**], slide over to I/O, and select Prompt

4. Hit [**ALPHA**] and the letters A,B,C,D. Hit [**ENTER**].

5. Put in the formula (A+C)/2. Then hit the [**STO**] button (right above the ON button). After the little arrow, hit [**ALPHA**] and type in an E. Hit [**ENTER**].

6. Put in the formula (B+D)/2. Then hit the [**STO**] button (right above the ON button). After the little arrow, hit [**ALPHA**] and type in an F. Hit [**ENTER**].

7. Go to [**PGRM**], slide over to I/O and choose Disp. Then put E, F.

8. Hit [**2nd**] and then [**MODE**] to quit setup. Go to [**PGRM**] and EXEC and choose it from your program list to use it.

WHAT YOUR SCREEN SHOULD LOOK LIKE WHEN PROGRAMMING

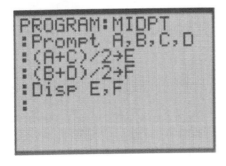

SEE IT ON A SAMPLE ACT QUESTION:

1. What is the midpoint of the line segment whose endpoints are (4,8) and (-2,24)?

A. (1, 12)

B. (1, 16)

C. (2, 8)

D. (2, 12)

E. (2, 16)

Note: Hit the [**PGRM**] button, select MIDPT, and you will be prompted for A, B, C, and D. Here, A = 4, B = 8, C = -2, and D = 24. The calculator will give you the midpoint: (1, 16). The answer choice is B.

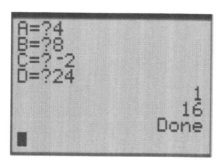

Do you have The Real ACT Prep Guide (2005 or 2007) or the free practice test from the ACT website (2009-2012)? Check out these opportunities to use this program:

Real ACT Prep Guide Test 3: #15

CHAPTER 9

Find the endpoint when given a midpoint and the other endpoint

You will occasionally be asked to find the endpoint of a line when given the midpoint and one of the endpoints. For this program, you will be prompted for MIDPT X, MIDPT Y, ENDPT X, and ENDPT Y. The calculator will give you the other endpoint. This program takes the most time to install, but stick with it. It really isn't as awful as it looks.

STEP-BY-STEP DIRECTIONS

1. Hit [**PGRM**] and slide over to select NEW. Hit [**ENTER**].

2. Give the new program a name like ENDPT and hit [**ENTER**]

3. Hit [**PGRM**], slide over to I/O, and select Input.

4. Hit [**ALPHA**] while you type in the following characters: "MIDPTX=", A

Here's how to find them:

- After you hit [**ALPHA**], the " is found above the + symbol

- The MIDPTX can be inputted by hitting [**ALPHA**] and the letters

- The = sign can be found by hitting [**2nd**] and then MATH.

- The comma is above the number 7

- The A can be found by hitting [**ALPHA**] and then the letter A

5. Hit [**ALPHA**] while you type in the following characters: "MIDPT**Y**=", B

6. Hit [**ALPHA**] while you type in the following characters: "ENDPTX=", C

7. Hit [**ALPHA**] while you type in the following characters: "ENDPT**Y**=", D

8. Put in the formula 2A-C. Then hit the [**STO**] button (right above the ON button). After the little arrow, hit [**ALPHA**] and type in an X. Hit [**ENTER**].

9. Put in the formula 2B-D. Then hit the [**STO**] button (right above the ON button). After the little arrow, hit [**ALPHA**] and type in a Y. Hit [**ENTER**].

10. Go to [**PGRM**], slide over to I/O and choose Disp. Then put X, Y

11. Hit [**2nd**] and then [**MODE**] to quit setup. Go to [**PGRM**] and EXEC and choose it from your program list to use it.

WHAT YOUR SCREEN SHOULD LOOK LIKE WHEN PROGRAMMING

Screen 1

```
PROGRAM:ENDPOINT
:Input "MIDPTX="
?A
:Input "MIDPTY="
?B
:Input "ENDPTX="
?C█
:Input "ENDPTY="
```

Screen 2

```
PROGRAM:ENDPOINT
?D
:2A-C→X
:2B-D→Y
:Disp X,Y
:
:
:█
```

SEE IT ON A SAMPLE ACT QUESTION:

1. In the standard (x,y) coordinate plane, point B with coordinates (-5,4) is the midpoint of line segment AC, and A has coordinates (7,3). What are the coordinates of point C?

A. (-17, 5)

B. (-12, −5)

C. (6, 3.5)

D. $(6, 2)$

E. $(12, 5)$

Note: Hit the [**PGRM**] button, select ENDPT, and you will be prompted for MIDPT X, MIDPT Y, ENDPT X, and ENDPT Y. Here, MIDPT X = -5, MIDPT Y = 4, ENDPT X = 7, and ENDPT Y = 3. The calculator will return the missing endpoint of the line segment: $(-17, 5)$. The correct answer is A.

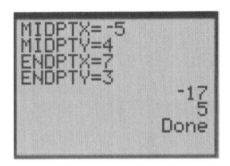

Do you have The Real ACT Prep Guide (2005 or 2007) or the free practice test from the ACT website (2009-2012)? Check out these opportunities to use this program:

Free practice test (on ACT website): #9

CHAPTER 10

Circumference of a circle

We haven't seen questions testing the circumference of a circle on the last several ACT tests. However, if you have trouble remembering the formula for the circumference of a circle, you may want to install this program just in case. This program will compute the circumference of a circle if you plug in the radius. **Please note that the program will calculate the numerical value of π and will give you a decimal answer.**

STEP-BY-STEP DIRECTIONS

1. Hit [**PGRM**] and slide over to select NEW. Hit [**ENTER**].

2. Give the new program a name like CCIRC and hit [**ENTER**]

3. Hit [**PGRM**], slide over to I/O, and select Prompt

4. Hit [**ALPHA**] and the letter R. Hit [**ENTER**].

5. Put in the formula $2\pi R$. Then hit the [**STO**] button (right above the ON button). After the little arrow, hit [**ALPHA**] and type in a C. Hit [**ENTER**].

6. Go to [**PGRM**], slide over to I/O and choose Disp. Then put a C.

7. Hit [**2nd**] and then [**MODE**] to quit setup. Go to [**PGRM**] and EXEC and choose it from your program list to use it.

WHAT YOUR SCREEN SHOULD LOOK LIKE WHEN PROGRAMMING

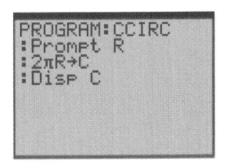

SEE IT ON A SAMPLE ACT QUESTION:

1. Doug's circular pool has a radius of 10 ft. Approximately how many feet of fencing would Doug need to construct a fence that completely surrounds the pool?

A. 21

B. 39

C. 63

D. 100

E. 186

Note: This is a circumference question in disguise.

If I hit the [**PGRM**] button and select the program CCIRC, I am prompted for R, the radius. The calculator then gives me the circumference of the circle – 62.83. The answer is C.

```
prgmCCIRC
R=?10
        62.83185307
              Done
■
```

PART II

Calculator Tips and Tricks

CHAPTER 11

The sneaky storage tip

Are you worried about remembering certain formulas? You can program your calculator to display a list of formulas for you when you need them on test day.

For example, let's say you are worried you'll forget the trig acronym SOHCAHTOA and the formula for finding the area of a triangle. Here are the step-by-step directions to program these into a special formula display program. Once you get the hang of it, you can input any formulas you want for reference.

STEP-BY-STEP DIRECTIONS

1. Hit [**PGRM**] and slide over to select NEW

2. Give the new program a name like FORMULA and hit [**ENTER**]

3. Hit [**PGRM**], slide over to I/O and select Disp. Hit [**ENTER**]

4. Select ["] (found above your + button)

5. Put in the formula you want displayed, like SOHCAHTOA.

6. Place another ["]. Hit [**ENTER**].

7. Keep doing this for any formulas you want displayed. (You can see our sample triangle area equation below). Remember that your = sign can be found by hitting [**2ⁿᵈ**] and then [**MATH**].

8. Hit [**2nd**] and then [**MODE**] to quit setup. Go to [**PGRM**] and EXEC and choose it from your program list to use it.

WHAT YOUR SCREEN SHOULD LOOK LIKE WHEN PROGRAMMING

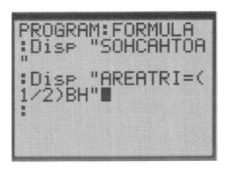

WHEN YOU RUN THE PROGRAM, IT WILL DISPLAY THE EQUATIONS YOU TOLD IT TO DISPLAY:

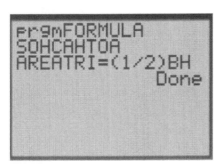

CHAPTER 12

Solving the matrix problem

There's usually one matrix problem on the ACT and usually, your calculator can easily solve it for you. As a reminder, a matrix problem looks like this:

What is the matrix product of $\begin{bmatrix} 2 \\ 6 \\ 0 \end{bmatrix} [1\ 0\ \text{-}1]$?

Good news! Your calculator can store many different matrices. You can then tell the calculator to perform whatever operation you want.

HERE'S HOW TO USE YOUR CALCULATOR TO SOLVE THIS PROBLEM.

1. Hit [**MATRX**]. Let's call our first matrix [A]. Slide over to EDIT for matrix [A].

2. Let the calculator know the dimensions of matrix A. Here, our first matrix, [A], is a 3 x 1 since there is one column with three rows. (The calculator will display the matrix format so you can see if you got this part right.)

3. Plug the numbers for the first matrix into your calculator.

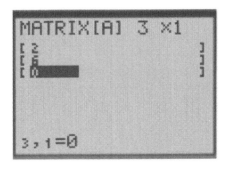

4. Go to MATRIX again and slide over to EDIT to edit your second matrix, matrix [B].

5. Let the calculator know the matrix's dimensions. Here, our second matrix, [B], is a 1 x 3 matrix since it has three columns and one row.

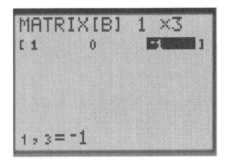

6. You've stored the matrices. Hit [**2nd**] and [**MODE**] to quit and return to your main screen.

Now you can perform any operations with your matrices. Since this question is asking for the product, we will multiply them.

7. Select MATRX and hit [**ENTER**] to select matrix [A].

8. Hit the multiplication button (the 'x') to indicate multiplication.

9. Select MATRX, scroll down to [B] and hit [**ENTER**] to select matrix [B].

10. Hit [**ENTER**]. You will see the product.

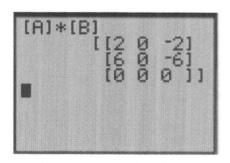

SEE IT ON A SAMPLE ACT QUESTION:

1. The number of students in elective classes at a certain high school can be represented by the following matrix.

Current events   Art studio   Music   Speech

[40   30   80   20]

The school principal estimates the ratio of the number of A grades that will be earned to the number of students enrolled in the classes with the following matrix.

Current events   [.2]

Art studio   [.2]

Music   [.3]

Speech   [.4]

Given these matrices, what is the principal's estimate for the amount of A's that will be earned in these elective classes?

A. 40

B. 42

C. 46

D. 49

E. 51

Note: this is a difficult problem, but you can tackle it using your calculator. Hit [**MATRX**] and store the two matrices in your calculator.

(Note that the 4th column is farther to the right and doesn't appear in the screenshot below)

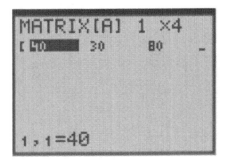

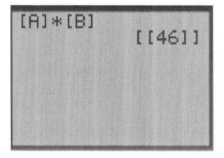

Now go ahead and multiply them.

```
[A]*[B]
           [[46]]
```

The correct answer is C.

Do you have The Real ACT Prep Guide (2005 or 2007) or the free practice test from the ACT website (2009-2012)? Check out these opportunities to use this program:

Free practice test (on ACT website): #11

Real ACT Prep Guide Test 1: #13

Real ACT Prep Guide Test 2: #42

CHAPTER 13

Finding the equation of a line/slope of a line when given 2 points

This isn't really a program. It's an easy 10 second calculator technique to find the equation (or just slope) when given two points. You've probably seen a question on the ACT or SAT testing this concept. Here's how to find it without the sloppy work.

Let's say you had two points, (5,2) and (3,8), and you wanted to find the slope of line passing through those points. Press STAT > 1:Edit... and enter the x-coordinates in L1, and the y-coordinates in L2. So L1={5 3} and L2={2 8}.

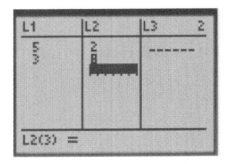

Then, go to [Stat] > Calc > 4:LinReg(ax+b) then press [**ENTER**] twice. You'll be shown the results of the linear regression. For this particular problem, you'll get results like this:

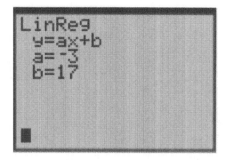

I don't know why the calculator chooses to use an 'a' instead of an 'm' when displaying the $y = mx + b$ equation. But in any case, the line here would be $y = -3x+17$. Since the -3 is in the 'm' spot in the $y = mx + b$ equation, the slope of the line is -3.

SEE IT ON A SAMPLE ACT QUESTION:

1. Find the equation of the straight line that passes through (-5, 2) and (4, -7).

A. y = 1x - 3

B. y = -1x + 3

C. y = -5x - 7

D. y = -1x +7

E. y = -1x – 3

Note: Go to STAT and Edit, and input the 2 points. Then head back to STAT, slide over to CALC, and scroll down to LinReg. You'll see an answer that says:

y = ax + b

a = -1

b = -3

Therefore, the equation of the line is y = -1x – 3. The answer is E.

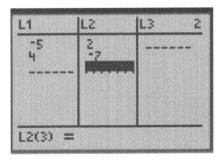

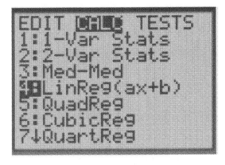

Do you have The Real ACT Prep Guide (2005 or 2007) or the free practice test from the ACT website (2009-2012)? Check out these opportunities to use this program:

Free practice test (on ACT website): #52

Real ACT Prep Guide Test 2: #16

CHAPTER 14

Finding the point where two lines intersect

This isn't really a program. It's an easy 10 second calculator technique to find where two lines intersect. You've probably seen a question on the ACT or SAT testing this concept. Here's how to find it without the sloppy work.

Let's say you wanted to find out where these two lines intersect:

$y = 2x+1$

$y = -1/2\,x + 6$

Input your equations by pressing the [**Y=**] button at the top left hand corner of the calculator.

Record each equation in the calculator. To calculate the intersection of the lines, hit [**2nd**] and CALC (located above the TRACE button) and scroll down to the option that says "intersect."

Hit [**ENTER**]. As you view the graph, press the [**ENTER**] button **three** times, and the points of intersection will appear in the lower left hand corner of your screen under the heading 'Intersection'.

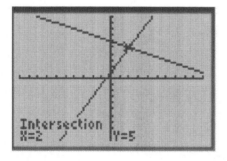

These two lines intersect at the point (2, 5).

SEE IT ON A SAMPLE ACT QUESTION:

1. What is the x coordinate of the point in the standard (x, y) coordinate plane at which the two lines y = 3x - 7 and y = -2x +3 intersect?

A. -1

B. 1

C. 2

D. 3

E. 7

Note: input both equations, hit [**2nd**] and CALC. Then scroll down to 'intersect' and make sure to hit [**ENTER**] three times until you see the word 'Intersection' along with the answer. The point of intersection here is (2, -1). Since this question is just asking for the x coordinate, the answer is C.

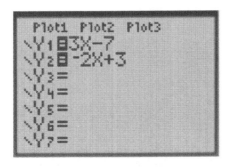

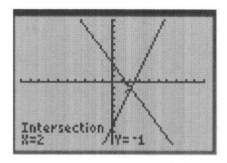

Do you have The Real ACT Prep Guide (2005 or 2007) or the free practice test from the ACT website (2009-2012)? Check out these opportunities to use this program:

Real ACT Prep Guide Test 1: #31

CHAPTER 15

Solving a system of equations (also called simultaneous equations)

This isn't really a program. It's an easy 15 second calculator technique to solve a system of equations. You've probably seen a question on the ACT testing this concept. Just to refresh your memory, here is an example of a system of equations:

$$2y = 4x + 2$$

$$4y = -2x + 24$$

Usually, you can solve such a system by substitution or combination. Depending on the complexity of the equations, using combination or substitution may take a lot of time and students often make careless mistakes. It's good to know that you can also solve this problem type with your calculator.

First, move your equations around or simplify them to get them into $y = mx + b$ form. The two equations above would now be $y = 2x+1$ and $y = -1/2\ x + 6$.

Now, just use the same calculator technique used to find the intersection of two lines. After all, these two lines will intersect at the point where both y's and x's are the same. And that's what solving a system of equations is about: finding the y and x shared by both lines. Here's what to do:

Graph your equations by pressing the [**Y=**] button at the top left hand corner of the calculator.

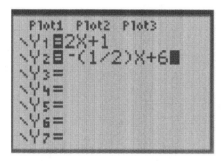

Record each equation in the calculator. To calculate the intersection of the lines, hit [**2nd**] and CALC (located above the TRACE button) and scroll down to the option that says "intersect."

Hit [**ENTER**]. As you view the graph, press the [**ENTER**] button **three** times, and the points of intersection will appear in the lower left hand corner of your screen under the heading 'Intersection'. If your graphs do not intersect, there is no value that solves the system of the equations.

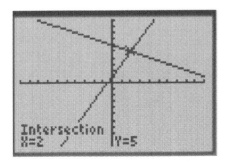

In the example above, plugging the equations into the calculator and calculating the intersection gives you x = 2, y = 5. Therefore, x = 2 and y = 5 are the solution to this system of equations.

SEE IT ON A SAMPLE ACT QUESTION:

1. In the system of linear equations below, what is the value of *y*?

-2x + 3y = 8

3x - y = -5

A. -1

B. 2

C. 4

D. 5

E. 6

Note: Again, you have several ways to solve this problem. If you don't want to combine or substitute, head to your TI 83 or 84. First rewrite the equations and input them into the calculator by hitting the $[\mathbf{Y}=]$ button:

$$y = (2/3)x + 8/3$$

$$y = 3x + 5$$

Then, hit $[\mathbf{2nd}]$ and $[\mathbf{CALC}]$. Scroll down to 'intersect.' Once you see the graph, hit $[\mathbf{ENTER}]$ three times and your calculator will give you the point of intersection, (-1, 2). The answer is B.

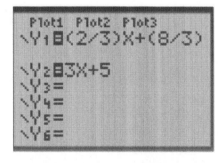

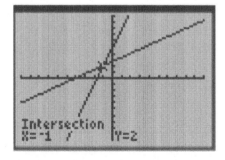

2. A test has twenty questions worth 100 points. The test consists of True/False questions worth 3 points each and multiple choice questions worth 8 points each. How many multiple choice questions are on the test?

A. 3

B. 6

C. 8

D. 12

E. 15

Note: Look out for word problems that are really testing your ability to solve systems of equations. You can solve this problem in many different ways – by substitution, combination, or working backward from the answer choices. Here's how to solve it using your calculator:

Create two equations that describe the problem above. Let's say we call the number of true/false questions x, and the number of multiple choice questions y.

$x + y = 20$

$3x + 8y = 100$

To use your calculator, solve for y:

$y = 20\text{-}x$

$y = (100/8) - (3/8)x$

Input the two equations into your calculator, hit [**2nd**] CALC, choose intersect, hit [**ENTER**] 3 times and you're done. (Yes, it's a mouthful – but it took longer to read it than to actually do it, right?) Since the lines intersect at x = 8, y = 12, the correct answer is C.

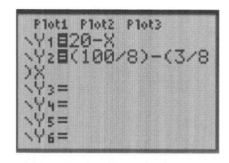

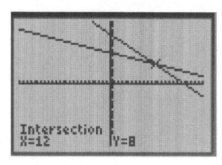

Do you have The Real ACT Prep Guide (2005 or 2007) or the free practice test from the ACT website (2009-2012)? Check out these opportunities to use this program:

Real ACT Prep Guide Test 2: #11

CHAPTER 16

Greatest common factor/ Least common multiple

Lately, we have noticed a few questions on the ACT that deal with finding factors and multiples of large, unwieldy numbers. You may remember that the greatest common factor (GCF) of two numbers is the largest number that divides into two (or more) numbers. For example, the GCF of 14 and 21 is 7. The least common multiple (LCM) is the smallest number that is a multiple of two numbers. For example, the LCM of 14 and 21 is 42.

How to do this on your calculator? Simple:

STEP-BY-STEP DIRECTIONS

1. Hit the MATH button and slide over to NUM

2. Depending on what you're being asked for, slide down to either 8: LCM or 9: GCD (*Note:* GCD stands for greatest common divisor – the same thing as a greatest common factor).

3. Enter the two numbers in the parenthesis, separated by a comma.

4. Press [**ENTER**]. Your calculator will display either the GCF or the LCM.

1. What is the greatest common factor of 18 and 282?

   A. 4

   B. 6

   C. 9

   D. 564

   E. 5076

Note: Since this question is asking for the GCF, hit the MATH button, slide over to NUM, and select GCD. Enter (18, 282) and hit [**ENTER**]. The calculator will display 6, the GCF of those two numbers. The answer is B.

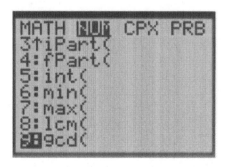

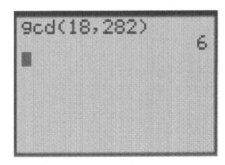

Do you have The Real ACT Prep Guide (2005 or 2007) or the free practice test from the ACT website (2009-2012)? Check out these opportunities to use this program:

Real ACT Prep Guide Test 3: #9 (to check answers)

= the ACT score of your dreams

Interested in ACT prep based on official ACT tests? Check out the ACT test prep software everyone's talking about!

Boost Your Score: The Unofficial Software Guide to the Real ACT offers:

- A comprehensive analysis of students' strengths and weaknesses based on performance on 4 real ACT tests (the free test on the ACT website and the 3 tests in The Real ACT Prep Guide*)

- Pinpoints the exact skills students need to improve

- Comprehensive review of all skills tested on the ACT

- Links to practice problems, quizzes, interactive worksheets, and tutorials to boost any skills needing improvement.

- Powerful, proven strategies for all ACT sections

Check us out on Amazon by searching for "Boost Your Score" or head to our website for quick digital download:

http://whatsyouradvantage.org/advantagepoint/boostyour-score.html

Good luck!!

*sold separately, or available at your library for free

advΛntagePoint

cutting edge test prep | painless prices

www.whatsyouradvantage.org

Made in the USA
Lexington, KY
24 February 2012